ONE
HUNDRED
WISHES

Other books by Rohan Candappa:

* No, hold on a minute, that was J. K. Rowling. Damn.
I suppose this means I'll have to send the Mercedes back.

ONE HUNDRED WISHES

BY ROHAN CANDAPPA

**Andrews McMeel
Publishing**

Kansas City

05 06 07 08 09 BID 10 9 8 7 6 5 4 3 2 1

ISBN: 0-7407-5018-6

Library of Congress Catalog Card Number: 2004111308

For my children, on their birthdays.
And every other day of their lives.
And for everyone else that I love.

Introduction

How many words do the Eskimos have for snow?
The thing is, we don't tell each other what we feel. Not really. Not often enough. We skirt around the subject. We hint at it. We comfort ourselves with the thought that the other person "knows how we feel about them." It might be a partner, a parent, or a child. But whoever it is, we expect them to know. Alternatively, we avoid the subject of feelings altogether. We shy away from sentiment, for fear of being sentimental. We save expressions of love for the heady realm of romance. Or the inadequate sign-off on a letter or a card. Or moments of crisis. And as for the love we hold for our friends, we are totally unequipped to express that in any way that adequately conveys just how much they mean to us.

The trouble is that "love" is a word that's been stretched to cover so much. We can say "I love my child" and we can say "I love those shoes." And in stretching the word so far, we have made it, in places, thin and brittle and prone to cracking. Until, when we do use the word, we run the risk of breaking it apart and finding ourselves standing knee-deep in the splintered shards of what we mean to say.

At which point my mind starts to wander off in envy to the Eskimos—the Eskimos who, rumor has it, have forty-nine words for snow. They have so many words because snow is so important to their culture, their way of life, their very being. So what does it say about us that we only have one word for love?

Then I got to thinking that maybe if the word "love" is too imprecise, too over used, too easily misunderstood to use freely, then maybe it's other words that we need. Other words and an occasion when we are allowed to express just a small part of what we feel. Even if we don't know how to do it.

Every year everybody has a birthday, and all we ever tend to say on such occasions is "Happy Birthday." It occurred to me that "Happy Birthday" is not enough, it's nowhere near enough, to express what I feel for the people I love. Of course, I do wish them a "Happy Birthday," but I wish them more than that. I wish them so much more than that.

R.L.C.

1 I wish you a shaft of sunlight on the gloomiest of days.

2 I wish you a kiss in the moonlight from someone you love.

3

I wish that no matter how much it rains your socks never get wet.

I **wish** that no one ever makes you eat brussels sprouts.

5 I wish you friends who love you
for who you are.

6 **I wish** you compassion.

7 I wish you the sound of your children's laughter.

8 **I wish** you the smell of new-mown grass.

9 I wish to retract the last wish if you suffer from hay fever.

10 **I wish** that you never fear failure, for doing so makes it hard to succeed.

11 I **wish** you the strength to see the
opportunities in your adversities.

12 I wish you a mountain to climb and the will to do it.

13 I **wish** you a big squashy sofa with a cat sleeping on its arm.

14 **I wish** that you meet someone who makes your heart race.

15 **I wish** that you learn to tread lightly on the earth.

16 **I wish** you the shade of a big tree on a sunny day.

17 **I wish** that you never have to stand in line for the ladies' room.

18 I wish you a love of learning.

19 I wish you the temperament to teach.

20 I wish that you never get caught in your zipper (or whatever the equivalent is for girls).

21 **I wish** that in restaurants you always choose the meal that everyone else wishes they'd ordered.

22 I wish you a kingfisher darting low over a stream.

23 I **wish** that no matter how venerable an age you attain, at least once a year you splash in a puddle.

24 I **wish** you a long lazy morning with breakfast in bed.

25 I wish you never end up with anyone who snores.

26 I **wish** that prejudice never taints your mind.

27 I wish you a home as welcoming as a mother's embrace.

28 I wish you a hill to roll down on a sunny day.

29 **I wish** that you see that beauty lies in the shadows as well as in the sun.

30 I wish you the love of reading and a book at your bedside every night.

31 **I wish** that you always remember to turn the iron off.

32 I wish you a dancing elephant.

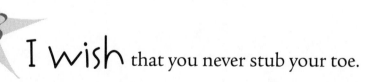

I wish that you never stub your toe.

34 I wish you hot meals on cold days.

35 I **wish** you cold drinks on hot days.

36 I wish you rainbows and fireworks.

37 I **wish** you grinches and gruffaloes.

38 I wish you a good memory, except for grievances.

39 **I wish** you the gaps between buildings and the worlds beyond that they reveal.

40 **I wish** you a good plumber and a reliable builder.

41 **I wish** that you know where the
fuse box is whenever the lights go out.

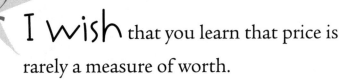

42 I **wish** that you learn that price is rarely a measure of worth.

43 I **wish** you self-knowledge
devoid of self-importance.

44 I **wish** that your gravy never goes lumpy.

45 I **wish** that the bag never splits
when you pull it out of the bin.

46 I wish you courage.

47 **I wish** you fear, for if you have never known fear how can you comfort those you love when they, too, are afraid?

48 I wish you ambition never tainted by arrogance.

49 **I wish** that you find your own path through the forest.

50 **I wish** you the sense to laugh at the world and all its absurdities and the wisdom to laugh at yourself before others do.

51 **I wish** you mistakes so that you can learn.

52 **I wish** you patience, because sometimes the world will insist on walking when you want to run.

53 **I wish** that you always find your size,
no matter how late you go to the sales.

54 I **wish** that once a year you ditch work early and go to see a movie in the afternoon.

55 **I wish** that no matter how many fancy restaurants you eat in you never lose the love of a good BLT sandwich.

56 I wish you the strength to face your fears, to recognize them as part of yourself, and still move on.

57 I wish you the wisdom to listen to the inarticulate.

58 I wish that you never lose the sustenance that is hope.

59 I wish that a small child falls asleep in your arms.

60 I wish you a garden on a summer's day where two squirrels play.

61 **I wish** you two magpies
wherever you go.

62 I wish you confidence.

63 **I** **wish** you doubt, because certainty is the comfort of tyrants.

64 I wish that your bread always lands buttered side up.

65 I wish that you're never the last to laugh.

66 **I wish** that whenever you draw you fill the page and use all the colors.

67 I wish you choices.

68 I wish you clouds that billow like dreams into the shapes of animals and islands.

69 **I wish** you the fluttering wings of hummingbirds to lullaby you to sleep.

70 I wish you passion.

I wish that when you're blessed with old age you have memories to feast on and a mind that's still hungry.

72 **I wish** that you're never too far from the next cake shop.

73 **I wish** that you always have the time to watch a hesitant raindrop wending its way down a window pane.

74 I wish you birdsong.

I wish that you remember all of us are flawed and that's okay.

I wish you heroes.

I **wish** that no matter how tall you walk, you never look down on those around you.

78 I wish you words that make you smile, like squelch, cous cous, and jojoba.

I wish that no matter how tall you walk, you never look down on those around you.

78 **I wish** you words that make you smile, like squelch, cous cous, and jojoba.

79 **I wish** that whatever skepticism you possess never darkens into cynicism.

80 I wish you a Tiger Woods bunker shot, a Nina Simone song, and a glass of Glenmorangie single malt Scotch.

81 I **wish** that your dealings with lawyers are mercifully brief.

82 I **wish** that you learn that we have two ears but only one mouth for a reason.

83 I **wish** you vision that lets you see
the good in others and the faults in yourself.

84 I wish you the abandon to dance badly at weddings.

85 I wish you always get a seat by the window.

86 I **wish** you a passport photo that your friends don't laugh at.

87 **I wish** that you always make enough dessert.

88 I wish you a boat on an ocean that races with dolphins.

89 I wish that you always help the woman with the buggy.

90 I wish that eventually you always find the missing sock.

91 **I wish** you laugh lines, not wrinkles.

92 **I wish** that even at your lowest ebb you know that my love is a turning tide that will always find you.

93 **I wish** that you always find money down the back of the sofa.

94 I **wish** you daffodils every spring, snowdrops every winter, and the bluest of cornflowers every summer.

95 I wish you snow on Christmas day.

96 I wish you the warmth of the beds that you slept in as a child.

97 I wish you curiosity.

98 **I wish** that you can feel my hand in yours whenever you need it.

99 **I wish** that you always have one wish left.

100

I wish...